# This Journal Belongs To:

_____

_____

# Welcome, Empath!
# You are a true superhero.

This journal was created by an empath for empaths. Even if you don't consider yourself an empath, you may be an intuitive or psychic with empathic tendencies. Being an empath can be a beautiful experience or a downright maddening curse. The biggest relief of the whole journey comes when you find out there's a name for 'what's wrong with you' and that it turns out, nothing is wrong with you at all. This gift can be a trick to manage, and this journal could be one of the many tools that you find helpful in navigating the choppy waters of being an empath.

In this book you will find prompted pages to help you unravel feelings, thoughts, emotions and situations that you encounter throughout your days. By journaling your experiences, you may uncover secrets to your own well-being. This can help to elevate your mood, determine where the feelings are coming from and uncover what you can do to provide yourself with some relief.

Enjoy the journey. No one else is going to do that part for you.

# How to Use this Book

Whenever you have an overwhelming feeling, sensitivity, triggered response or emotion, it's helpful to dissect the wheres, whats and whys. This can help you to manage your powers more easily as situations arise.

Write about the following:

**The feeling: is it emotional, physical, mental?** What or who triggered it?

**Is the feeling even yours?** As an empath, many of the feelings, emotions, sensitivities and reactions you experience may be picked up from others. Some empaths are very good at personalizing all feelings (and there's a good use for that talent as well) but if you can determine what's yours and what is not, that can be incredibly helpful.

**Synchronicities and associations:** regarding the situation you're writing about, record any synchronicities that were present or any associations with past feelings, people, voices or situations. This can help you to unravel what you're feeling and what to do about it.

# Self-Care

The all-important and 100% necessary activity that empaths must find a way to work into their lives is **self-care**.

There are many wonderful and informative books, articles and workshop courses available to help you determine effective ways to put yourself first and achieve self-care. Here are a few to get you started:

1. **Do the inner work.** If you are faced with a situation that is yours and has many past associations that came along with it, look lovingly within to unravel the nonsense associated with that feeling so that you can carry on without the weight of unnecessary burdens.

2. **Create boundaries.** So important. Say no when your inner guidance doesn't feel joyful. Separate yourself from toxic or negative relationships. Empower yourself with positive reinforcement as you step into the perfect being that you've always been.

3. **Don't be a victim.** Victim consciousness is another topic all by itself, but empaths often find a life before them that points straight to it. Don't be a victim. You're not a victim. You just haven't found your amazingness yet. Look for it. It's within you.

4. **Be nice to yourself.** Always. Every minute of every day. Don't rely on anything outside of you to take care of this. Give yourself gifts, compliments and engage in activities that lift your spirits.

Date:

Is the feeling Physical - Emotional - Mental

Describe the feeling: _____

_____

_____

_____

_____

_____

What was the trigger?: _____

_____

_____

_____

_____

Is it mine?: _____

_____

_____

_____

_____

Synchronicities and Associations: _____

_____
_____
_____
_____

Inner work I can do: _____

_____
_____
_____
_____
_____
_____
_____

Self-Care Practiced: _____

_____
_____
_____
_____
_____

Date:

Is the feeling Physical - Emotional - Mental

Describe the feeling: _____

_____
_____
_____
_____
_____
_____

What was the trigger?: _____

_____
_____
_____
_____

Is it mine?: _____

_____
_____
_____
_____

Synchronicities and Associations: _____

_____
_____
_____
_____

Inner work I can do: _____

_____
_____
_____
_____
_____
_____
_____

Self-Care Practiced: _____

_____
_____
_____
_____
_____
_____

Date:

Is the feeling Physical - Emotional - Mental

Describe the feeling: _____

_____

_____

_____

_____

_____

_____

What was the trigger?: _____

_____

_____

_____

_____

Is it mine?: _____

_____

_____

_____

_____

Synchronicities and Associations: _____

_____
_____
_____
_____

Inner work I can do: _____

_____
_____
_____
_____
_____
_____
_____

Self-Care Practiced: _____

_____
_____
_____
_____
_____
_____

Date:

Is the feeling Physical - Emotional - Mental

Describe the feeling: _____

_____

_____

_____

_____

_____

_____

What was the trigger?: _____

_____

_____

_____

_____

Is it mine?: _____

_____

_____

_____

_____

Synchronicities and Associations: _____

_____
_____
_____
_____

Inner work I can do: _____

_____
_____
_____
_____
_____
_____

Self-Care Practiced: _____

_____
_____
_____
_____
_____
_____

Date:

Is the feeling Physical - Emotional - Mental

Describe the feeling: _____

_____

_____

_____

_____

_____

What was the trigger?: _____

_____

_____

_____

Is it mine?: _____

_____

_____

_____

Synchronicities and Associations: _____

_____

_____

_____

_____


Inner work I can do: _____

_____

_____

_____

_____

_____

_____


Self-Care Practiced: _____

_____

_____

_____

_____

_____

_____

Date:

Is the feeling Physical - Emotional - Mental

Describe the feeling: _____

_____

_____

_____

_____

_____

_____


What was the trigger?: _____

_____

_____

_____

_____


Is it mine?: _____

_____

_____

_____

_____

Synchronicities and Associations: _____

_____

_____

_____

_____

Inner work I can do: _____

_____

_____

_____

_____

_____

_____

_____

Self-Care Practiced: _____

_____

_____

_____

_____

_____

_____

Date:

Is the feeling Physical - Emotional - Mental

Describe the feeling: _____

_____

_____

_____

_____

_____

_____

What was the trigger?: _____

_____

_____

_____

_____

Is it mine?: _____

_____

_____

_____

_____

Synchronicities and Associations: _____

_____
_____
_____
_____

Inner work I can do: _____

_____
_____
_____
_____
_____
_____
_____

Self-Care Practiced: _____

_____
_____
_____
_____
_____
_____

Date:

Is the feeling Physical - Emotional - Mental

Describe the feeling: _____

_____

_____

_____

_____

_____

What was the trigger?: _____

_____

_____

_____

Is it mine?: _____

_____

_____

_____

Synchronicities and Associations: _____

_____
_____
_____
_____

Inner work I can do: _____

_____
_____
_____
_____
_____
_____

Self-Care Practiced: _____

_____
_____
_____
_____
_____
_____

Date:

Is the feeling Physical - Emotional - Mental

Describe the feeling: _____

_____

_____

_____

_____

_____

_____

What was the trigger?: _____

_____

_____

_____

_____

Is it mine?: _____

_____

_____

_____

_____

Synchronicities and Associations: _____

_____
_____
_____
_____

Inner work I can do: _____

_____
_____
_____
_____
_____
_____
_____
_____

Self-Care Practiced: _____

_____
_____
_____
_____
_____
_____

Date:

Is the feeling Physical - Emotional - Mental

Describe the feeling: _____
_____
_____
_____
_____
_____
_____

What was the trigger?: _____
_____
_____
_____
_____

Is it mine?: _____
_____
_____
_____
_____

Synchronicities and Associations: _____

_____
_____
_____
_____

Inner work I can do: _____

_____
_____
_____
_____
_____
_____
_____

Self-Care Practiced: _____

_____
_____
_____
_____
_____
_____

Date:

Is the feeling Physical - Emotional - Mental

Describe the feeling: _____

_____

_____

_____

_____

_____

_____

What was the trigger?: _____

_____

_____

_____

_____

Is it mine?: _____

_____

_____

_____

_____

Synchronicities and Associations: _____

_____

_____

_____

_____

Inner work I can do: _____

_____

_____

_____

_____

_____

_____

_____

Self-Care Practiced: _____

_____

_____

_____

_____

_____

_____

Date:

Is the feeling Physical - Emotional - Mental

Describe the feeling: _____

_____

_____

_____

_____

_____

What was the trigger?: _____

_____

_____

_____

_____

Is it mine?: _____

_____

_____

_____

_____

Synchronicities and Associations: _____

_____

_____

_____

_____

Inner work I can do: _____

_____

_____

_____

_____

_____

_____

Self-Care Practiced: _____

_____

_____

_____

_____

_____

_____

Date:

Is the feeling Physical - Emotional - Mental

Describe the feeling: _____

_____

_____

_____

_____

_____

_____

What was the trigger?: _____

_____

_____

_____

_____

Is it mine?: _____

_____

_____

_____

_____

Synchronicities and Associations: _____

_____
_____
_____
_____

Inner work I can do: _____

_____
_____
_____
_____
_____
_____
_____

Self-Care Practiced: _____

_____
_____
_____
_____
_____
_____

Date:

Is the feeling Physical - Emotional - Mental

Describe the feeling: _____

_____

_____

_____

_____

_____

_____

What was the trigger?: _____

_____

_____

_____

_____

Is it mine?: _____

_____

_____

_____

_____

Synchronicities and Associations: _____

_____

_____

_____

_____


Inner work I can do: _____

_____

_____

_____

_____

_____

_____


Self-Care Practiced: _____

_____

_____

_____

_____

_____

Date:

Is the feeling Physical - Emotional - Mental

Describe the feeling: _____

_____

_____

_____

_____

_____

_____

What was the trigger?: _____

_____

_____

_____

_____

Is it mine?: _____

_____

_____

_____

_____

Synchronicities and Associations: _____

_____
_____
_____
_____

Inner work I can do: _____

_____
_____
_____
_____
_____
_____
_____

Self-Care Practiced: _____

_____
_____
_____
_____
_____
_____

Date:

Is the feeling Physical - Emotional - Mental

Describe the feeling: _____

_____
_____
_____
_____
_____
_____

What was the trigger?: _____

_____
_____
_____
_____

Is it mine?: _____

_____
_____
_____
_____

Synchronicities and Associations: _____

_____

_____

_____

_____

Inner work I can do: _____

_____

_____

_____

_____

_____

_____

_____

Self-Care Practiced: _____

_____

_____

_____

_____

_____

_____

Date:

Is the feeling Physical - Emotional - Mental

Describe the feeling: _____

_____

_____

_____

_____

_____

_____

What was the trigger?: _____

_____

_____

_____

_____

Is it mine?: _____

_____

_____

_____

_____

Synchronicities and Associations: _____

_____
_____
_____
_____

Inner work I can do: _____

_____
_____
_____
_____
_____
_____
_____

Self-Care Practiced: _____

_____
_____
_____
_____
_____
_____

Date:

Is the feeling Physical - Emotional - Mental

Describe the feeling: _____

_____

_____

_____

_____

_____

What was the trigger?: _____

_____

_____

_____

_____

Is it mine?: _____

_____

_____

_____

_____

Synchronicities and Associations: _____

_____
_____
_____
_____

Inner work I can do: _____

_____
_____
_____
_____
_____
_____

Self-Care Practiced: _____

_____
_____
_____
_____
_____
_____

Date:

Is the feeling Physical - Emotional - Mental

Describe the feeling: _____

_____

_____

_____

_____

_____

_____

What was the trigger?: _____

_____

_____

_____

_____

Is it mine?: _____

_____

_____

_____

_____

Synchronicities and Associations: _____

_____
_____
_____
_____

Inner work I can do: _____

_____
_____
_____
_____
_____
_____
_____

Self-Care Practiced: _____

_____
_____
_____
_____
_____
_____

Date:

Is the feeling Physical - Emotional - Mental

Describe the feeling: _____

_____

_____

_____

_____

_____

What was the trigger?: _____

_____

_____

_____

Is it mine?: _____

_____

_____

_____

Synchronicities and Associations: _____

_____
_____
_____
_____

Inner work I can do: _____

_____
_____
_____
_____
_____
_____
_____

Self-Care Practiced: _____

_____
_____
_____
_____
_____
_____

Date:

Is the feeling Physical - Emotional - Mental

Describe the feeling: _____

_____

_____

_____

_____

_____

What was the trigger?: _____

_____

_____

_____

_____

Is it mine?: _____

_____

_____

_____

_____

Synchronicities and Associations: _____

_____

_____

_____

_____

Inner work I can do: _____

_____

_____

_____

_____

_____

_____

_____

Self-Care Practiced: _____

_____

_____

_____

_____

_____

_____

Date:

Is the feeling Physical - Emotional - Mental

Describe the feeling: _____

_____

_____

_____

_____

_____

What was the trigger?: _____

_____

_____

_____

Is it mine?: _____

_____

_____

_____

Synchronicities and Associations: _____

_____
_____
_____
_____

Inner work I can do: _____

_____
_____
_____
_____
_____
_____
_____

Self-Care Practiced: _____

_____
_____
_____
_____
_____
_____

Date:

Is the feeling Physical - Emotional - Mental

Describe the feeling: _____

_____

_____

_____

_____

_____

_____

What was the trigger?: _____

_____

_____

_____

_____

Is it mine?: _____

_____

_____

_____

_____

Synchronicities and Associations: _____

_____

_____

_____

_____

Inner work I can do: _____

_____

_____

_____

_____

_____

_____

_____

Self-Care Practiced: _____

_____

_____

_____

_____

_____

_____

Date:

Is the feeling Physical - Emotional - Mental

Describe the feeling: _____

_____

_____

_____

_____

_____

_____

What was the trigger?: _____

_____

_____

_____

_____

Is it mine?: _____

_____

_____

_____

_____

Synchronicities and Associations: _____

_____
_____
_____
_____

Inner work I can do: _____

_____
_____
_____
_____
_____
_____
_____

Self-Care Practiced: _____

_____
_____
_____
_____
_____
_____

Date:

Is the feeling Physical - Emotional - Mental

Describe the feeling: _____

_____

_____

_____

_____

_____

What was the trigger?: _____

_____

_____

_____

_____

Is it mine?: _____

_____

_____

_____

_____

Synchronicities and Associations: _____

_____

_____

_____

_____

Inner work I can do: _____

_____

_____

_____

_____

_____

_____

_____

Self-Care Practiced: _____

_____

_____

_____

_____

_____

_____

Date:

Is the feeling Physical - Emotional - Mental

Describe the feeling: _____

_____

_____

_____

_____

_____

_____

What was the trigger?: _____

_____

_____

_____

_____

Is it mine?: _____

_____

_____

_____

_____

Synchronicities and Associations: _____

_____
_____
_____
_____

Inner work I can do: _____

_____
_____
_____
_____
_____
_____
_____

Self-Care Practiced: _____

_____
_____
_____
_____
_____
_____

Date:

Is the feeling Physical - Emotional - Mental

Describe the feeling: _____

_____

_____

_____

_____

_____

What was the trigger?: _____

_____

_____

_____

Is it mine?: _____

_____

_____

_____

_____

Synchronicities and Associations: _____

_____

_____

_____

_____

Inner work I can do: _____

_____

_____

_____

_____

_____

_____

_____

Self-Care Practiced: _____

_____

_____

_____

_____

_____

_____

Date:

Is the feeling Physical - Emotional - Mental

Describe the feeling: _____

_____

_____

_____

_____

_____

_____

What was the trigger?: _____

_____

_____

_____

_____

Is it mine?: _____

_____

_____

_____

_____

Synchronicities and Associations: _____

_____

_____

_____

_____

Inner work I can do: _____

_____

_____

_____

_____

_____

_____

_____

Self-Care Practiced: _____

_____

_____

_____

_____

_____

_____

Date:

Is the feeling Physical - Emotional - Mental

Describe the feeling: _____

_____

_____

_____

_____

_____

_____

What was the trigger?: _____

_____

_____

_____

_____

Is it mine?: _____

_____

_____

_____

_____

Synchronicities and Associations: _____

_____

_____

_____

_____

Inner work I can do: _____

_____

_____

_____

_____

_____

_____

_____

Self-Care Practiced: _____

_____

_____

_____

_____

_____

_____

Date:

Is the feeling Physical - Emotional - Mental

Describe the feeling: _____

_____

_____

_____

_____

_____

_____

What was the trigger?: _____

_____

_____

_____

_____

Is it mine?: _____

_____

_____

_____

_____

Synchronicities and Associations: _____

_____
_____
_____
_____

Inner work I can do: _____

_____
_____
_____
_____
_____
_____
_____

Self-Care Practiced: _____

_____
_____
_____
_____
_____
_____

Date:

Is the feeling Physical - Emotional - Mental

Describe the feeling: _____

_____

_____

_____

_____

_____

_____

What was the trigger?: _____

_____

_____

_____

_____

Is it mine?: _____

_____

_____

_____

_____

Synchronicities and Associations: _____

_____

_____

_____

_____

Inner work I can do: _____

_____

_____

_____

_____

_____

_____

_____

Self-Care Practiced: _____

_____

_____

_____

_____

_____

_____

Date:

Is the feeling Physical - Emotional - Mental

Describe the feeling: _____

_____

_____

_____

_____

_____

What was the trigger?: _____

_____

_____

_____

_____

Is it mine?: _____

_____

_____

_____

_____

Synchronicities and Associations: _____

_____
_____
_____
_____

Inner work I can do: _____

_____
_____
_____
_____
_____
_____
_____

Self-Care Practiced: _____

_____
_____
_____
_____
_____
_____

Date:

Is the feeling Physical - Emotional - Mental

Describe the feeling: _____

_____

_____

_____

_____

_____

_____

What was the trigger?: _____

_____

_____

_____

_____

Is it mine?: _____

_____

_____

_____

_____

Synchronicities and Associations: _____

_____
_____
_____
_____

Inner work I can do: _____

_____
_____
_____
_____
_____
_____
_____

Self-Care Practiced: _____

_____
_____
_____
_____
_____
_____

Date:

Is the feeling Physical - Emotional - Mental

Describe the feeling: _____

_____

_____

_____

_____

_____

_____

What was the trigger?: _____

_____

_____

_____

_____

Is it mine?: _____

_____

_____

_____

_____

Synchronicities and Associations: _____

_____
_____
_____
_____

Inner work I can do: _____

_____
_____
_____
_____
_____
_____
_____

Self-Care Practiced: _____

_____
_____
_____
_____
_____
_____

Date:

Is the feeling Physical - Emotional - Mental

Describe the feeling: _____

_____

_____

_____

_____

_____

_____

What was the trigger?: _____

_____

_____

_____

_____

Is it mine?: _____

_____

_____

_____

_____

Synchronicities and Associations: _____

_____
_____
_____
_____

Inner work I can do: _____

_____
_____
_____
_____
_____
_____
_____

Self-Care Practiced: _____

_____
_____
_____
_____
_____
_____

Date:

Is the feeling Physical - Emotional - Mental

Describe the feeling: _____

_____

_____

_____

_____

_____

_____

What was the trigger?: _____

_____

_____

_____

_____

Is it mine?: _____

_____

_____

_____

_____

Synchronicities and Associations: _____

_____
_____
_____
_____

Inner work I can do: _____

_____
_____
_____
_____
_____
_____
_____

Self-Care Practiced: _____

_____
_____
_____
_____
_____
_____

Date:

Is the feeling Physical - Emotional - Mental

Describe the feeling: _____

_____

_____

_____

_____

_____

What was the trigger?: _____

_____

_____

_____

_____

Is it mine?: _____

_____

_____

_____

_____

Synchronicities and Associations: _____

_____

_____

_____

_____

Inner work I can do: _____

_____

_____

_____

_____

_____

_____

_____

Self-Care Practiced: _____

_____

_____

_____

_____

_____

_____

Date:

Is the feeling Physical - Emotional - Mental

Describe the feeling: _____

_____

_____

_____

_____

_____

What was the trigger?: _____

_____

_____

_____

_____

Is it mine?: _____

_____

_____

_____

_____

Synchronicities and Associations: _____

_____

_____

_____

_____

Inner work I can do: _____

_____

_____

_____

_____

_____

_____

_____

Self-Care Practiced: _____

_____

_____

_____

_____

_____

_____

Date:

Is the feeling Physical - Emotional - Mental

Describe the feeling: _____

_____
_____
_____
_____
_____
_____

What was the trigger?: _____

_____
_____
_____
_____

Is it mine?: _____

_____
_____
_____
_____

Synchronicities and Associations: _____

_____

_____

_____

_____

Inner work I can do: _____

_____

_____

_____

_____

_____

_____

_____

Self-Care Practiced: _____

_____

_____

_____

_____

_____

_____

Date:

Is the feeling Physical - Emotional - Mental

Describe the feeling: _____

_____

_____

_____

_____

_____

What was the trigger?: _____

_____

_____

_____

_____

Is it mine?: _____

_____

_____

_____

_____

Synchronicities and Associations: _____

_____
_____
_____
_____

Inner work I can do: _____

_____
_____
_____
_____
_____
_____
_____

Self-Care Practiced: _____

_____
_____
_____
_____
_____
_____

Date:

Is the feeling Physical - Emotional - Mental

Describe the feeling: _____

_____

_____

_____

_____

_____

_____

What was the trigger?: _____

_____

_____

_____

_____

Is it mine?: _____

_____

_____

_____

_____

Synchronicities and Associations: _____

_____
_____
_____
_____

Inner work I can do: _____

_____
_____
_____
_____
_____
_____
_____

Self-Care Practiced: _____

_____
_____
_____
_____
_____
_____

Date:

Is the feeling Physical - Emotional - Mental

Describe the feeling: _____

_____

_____

_____

_____

_____

What was the trigger?: _____

_____

_____

_____

Is it mine?: _____

_____

_____

_____

_____

Synchronicities and Associations: _____

_____

_____

_____

_____

Inner work I can do: _____

_____

_____

_____

_____

_____

_____

_____

Self-Care Practiced: _____

_____

_____

_____

_____

_____

_____

Date:

Is the feeling Physical - Emotional - Mental

Describe the feeling: _____

_____

_____

_____

_____

_____

What was the trigger?: _____

_____

_____

_____

_____

Is it mine?: _____

_____

_____

_____

_____

Synchronicities and Associations: _____

_____
_____
_____
_____

Inner work I can do: _____

_____
_____
_____
_____
_____
_____
_____

Self-Care Practiced: _____

_____
_____
_____
_____
_____
_____

Date:

Is the feeling Physical - Emotional - Mental

Describe the feeling: _____

_____

_____

_____

_____

_____

What was the trigger?: _____

_____

_____

_____

Is it mine?: _____

_____

_____

_____

Synchronicities and Associations: _____

_____
_____
_____
_____

Inner work I can do: _____

_____
_____
_____
_____
_____
_____
_____

Self-Care Practiced: _____

_____
_____
_____
_____
_____
_____

Date:

Is the feeling Physical - Emotional - Mental

Describe the feeling: _____

_____

_____

_____

_____

_____

_____

What was the trigger?: _____

_____

_____

_____

_____

Is it mine?: _____

_____

_____

_____

_____

Synchronicities and Associations: _____

_____
_____
_____
_____

Inner work I can do: _____

_____
_____
_____
_____
_____
_____
_____

Self-Care Practiced: _____

_____
_____
_____
_____
_____
_____

Date:

Is the feeling Physical - Emotional - Mental

Describe the feeling: _____

_____

_____

_____

_____

_____

What was the trigger?: _____

_____

_____

_____

_____

Is it mine?: _____

_____

_____

_____

_____

Synchronicities and Associations: _____

_____
_____
_____
_____

Inner work I can do: _____

_____
_____
_____
_____
_____
_____
_____

Self-Care Practiced: _____

_____
_____
_____
_____
_____
_____

Date:

Is the feeling Physical - Emotional - Mental

Describe the feeling: _____

_____

_____

_____

_____

_____

_____

What was the trigger?: _____

_____

_____

_____

_____

Is it mine?: _____

_____

_____

_____

_____

Synchronicities and Associations: _____

_____

_____

_____

_____

Inner work I can do: _____

_____

_____

_____

_____

_____

_____

_____

Self-Care Practiced: _____

_____

_____

_____

_____

_____

_____

Date:

Is the feeling Physical - Emotional - Mental

Describe the feeling: _____

_____

_____

_____

_____

_____

_____

What was the trigger?: _____

_____

_____

_____

_____

Is it mine?: _____

_____

_____

_____

_____

Synchronicities and Associations: _____

_____
_____
_____
_____

Inner work I can do: _____

_____
_____
_____
_____
_____
_____
_____

Self-Care Practiced: _____

_____
_____
_____
_____
_____
_____

Date:

Is the feeling Physical - Emotional - Mental

Describe the feeling: _____

_____

_____

_____

_____

_____

_____

What was the trigger?: _____

_____

_____

_____

_____

Is it mine?: _____

_____

_____

_____

_____

Synchronicities and Associations: _____

_____
_____
_____
_____

Inner work I can do: _____

_____
_____
_____
_____
_____
_____
_____

Self-Care Practiced: _____

_____
_____
_____
_____
_____
_____

Date:

Is the feeling Physical - Emotional - Mental

Describe the feeling: _____

_____

_____

_____

_____

_____

What was the trigger?: _____

_____

_____

_____

Is it mine?: _____

_____

_____

_____

Synchronicities and Associations: _____

_____

_____

_____

_____

Inner work I can do: _____

_____

_____

_____

_____

_____

_____

_____

Self-Care Practiced: _____

_____

_____

_____

_____

_____

_____

Date:

Is the feeling Physical - Emotional - Mental

Describe the feeling: _____

_____

_____

_____

_____

_____

_____

What was the trigger?: _____

_____

_____

_____

_____

Is it mine?: _____

_____

_____

_____

_____

Synchronicities and Associations: _____

_____
_____
_____
_____

Inner work I can do: _____

_____
_____
_____
_____
_____
_____
_____

Self-Care Practiced: _____

_____
_____
_____
_____
_____
_____

Date:

Is the feeling Physical - Emotional - Mental

Describe the feeling: _____

_____

_____

_____

_____

_____

What was the trigger?: _____

_____

_____

_____

_____

Is it mine?: _____

_____

_____

_____

_____

Synchronicities and Associations: _____

_____

_____

_____

_____

Inner work I can do: _____

_____

_____

_____

_____

_____

_____

_____

Self-Care Practiced: _____

_____

_____

_____

_____

_____

_____

Date:

Is the feeling Physical - Emotional - Mental

Describe the feeling: _____

_____
_____
_____
_____
_____
_____

What was the trigger?: _____

_____
_____
_____
_____

Is it mine?: _____

_____
_____
_____
_____

Synchronicities and Associations: _____

_____
_____
_____
_____

Inner work I can do: _____

_____
_____
_____
_____
_____
_____
_____

Self-Care Practiced: _____

_____
_____
_____
_____
_____
_____

Date:

Is the feeling Physical - Emotional - Mental

Describe the feeling: _____

_____

_____

_____

_____

_____

_____

What was the trigger?: _____

_____

_____

_____

_____

Is it mine?: _____

_____

_____

_____

_____

Synchronicities and Associations: _____

_____
_____
_____
_____

Inner work I can do: _____

_____
_____
_____
_____
_____
_____
_____

Self-Care Practiced: _____

_____
_____
_____
_____
_____
_____

Date:

Is the feeling Physical - Emotional - Mental

Describe the feeling: _____

_____

_____

_____

_____

_____

_____

What was the trigger?: _____

_____

_____

_____

_____

Is it mine?: _____

_____

_____

_____

_____

Synchronicities and Associations: _____

_____
_____
_____
_____

Inner work I can do: _____

_____
_____
_____
_____
_____
_____
_____

Self-Care Practiced: _____

_____
_____
_____
_____
_____
_____

Date:

Is the feeling Physical - Emotional - Mental

Describe the feeling: _____

_____
_____
_____
_____
_____
_____

What was the trigger?: _____

_____
_____
_____
_____

Is it mine?: _____

_____
_____
_____
_____

Synchronicities and Associations: _____

_____
_____
_____
_____

Inner work I can do: _____

_____
_____
_____
_____
_____
_____
_____

Self-Care Practiced: _____

_____
_____
_____
_____
_____
_____

Date:

Is the feeling Physical - Emotional - Mental

Describe the feeling: _____

_____

_____

_____

_____

_____

_____

What was the trigger?: _____

_____

_____

_____

_____

Is it mine?: _____

_____

_____

_____

_____

Synchronicities and Associations: _____

_____
_____
_____
_____

Inner work I can do: _____

_____
_____
_____
_____
_____
_____
_____

Self-Care Practiced: _____

_____
_____
_____
_____
_____
_____

Date:

Is the feeling Physical - Emotional - Mental

Describe the feeling: _____

_____

_____

_____

_____

_____

_____

What was the trigger?: _____

_____

_____

_____

_____

Is it mine?: _____

_____

_____

_____

_____

Synchronicities and Associations: _____

_____
_____
_____
_____

Inner work I can do: _____

_____
_____
_____
_____
_____
_____
_____

Self-Care Practiced: _____

_____
_____
_____
_____
_____
_____

Date:

Is the feeling Physical - Emotional - Mental

Describe the feeling: _____

_____

_____

_____

_____

_____

_____

What was the trigger?: _____

_____

_____

_____

_____

Is it mine?: _____

_____

_____

_____

_____

Synchronicities and Associations: _____

_____
_____
_____
_____

Inner work I can do: _____

_____
_____
_____
_____
_____
_____
_____

Self-Care Practiced: _____

_____
_____
_____
_____
_____
_____

Date:

Is the feeling Physical - Emotional - Mental

Describe the feeling: _____

_____

_____

_____

_____

_____

What was the trigger?: _____

_____

_____

_____

Is it mine?: _____

_____

_____

_____

Synchronicities and Associations: _____

_____
_____
_____
_____

Inner work I can do: _____

_____
_____
_____
_____
_____
_____
_____

Self-Care Practiced: _____

_____
_____
_____
_____
_____
_____

Date:

Is the feeling Physical - Emotional - Mental

Describe the feeling: _____

_____

_____

_____

_____

_____

What was the trigger?: _____

_____

_____

_____

_____

Is it mine?: _____

_____

_____

_____

_____

Synchronicities and Associations: _____

_____
_____
_____
_____

Inner work I can do: _____

_____
_____
_____
_____
_____
_____
_____

Self-Care Practiced: _____

_____
_____
_____
_____
_____
_____
_____

Date:

Is the feeling Physical - Emotional - Mental

Describe the feeling: _____

_____

_____

_____

_____

_____

What was the trigger?: _____

_____

_____

_____

_____

Is it mine?: _____

_____

_____

_____

_____

Made in the USA
Las Vegas, NV
02 February 2022

42864435R00072